THE ESSENTIAL COLLECTION

FAURÉ

GOLD

Published by:
Chester Music Limited,
8/9 Frith Street, London W1D 3JB, England.

Order No. CH68662
ISBN 978-0-8256-3344-7
This book © Copyright 2005 by Chester Music.

Compiled by Michael Ahmad.
Music engraved by Camden Music.

Printed in the United States of America.

EXCLUSIVELY DISTRIBUTED BY

Après un rêve
Op.7, No.1
Composed by Gabriel Fauré

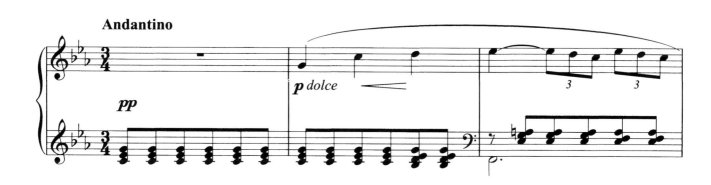

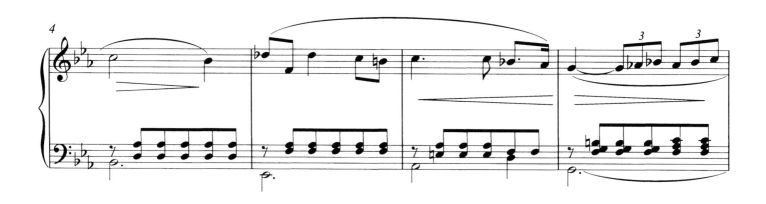

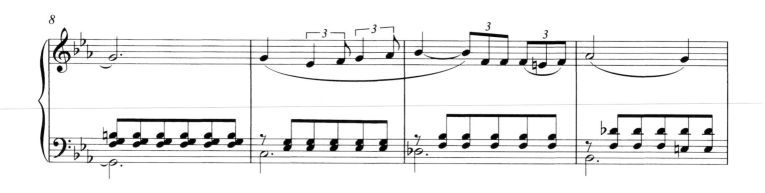

Chanson d'amour
Op.27, No.1

Composed by Gabriel Fauré

Clair de lune
Op.46, No.2

Composed by Gabriel Fauré

Andantino quasi allegretto $\quad \downarrow = 78$

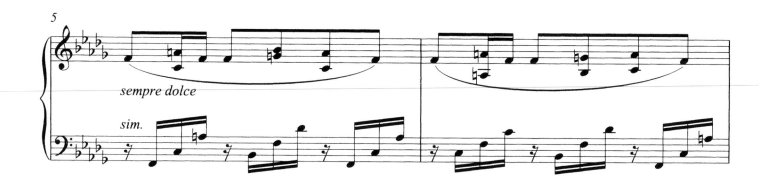

sempre dolce

sim.

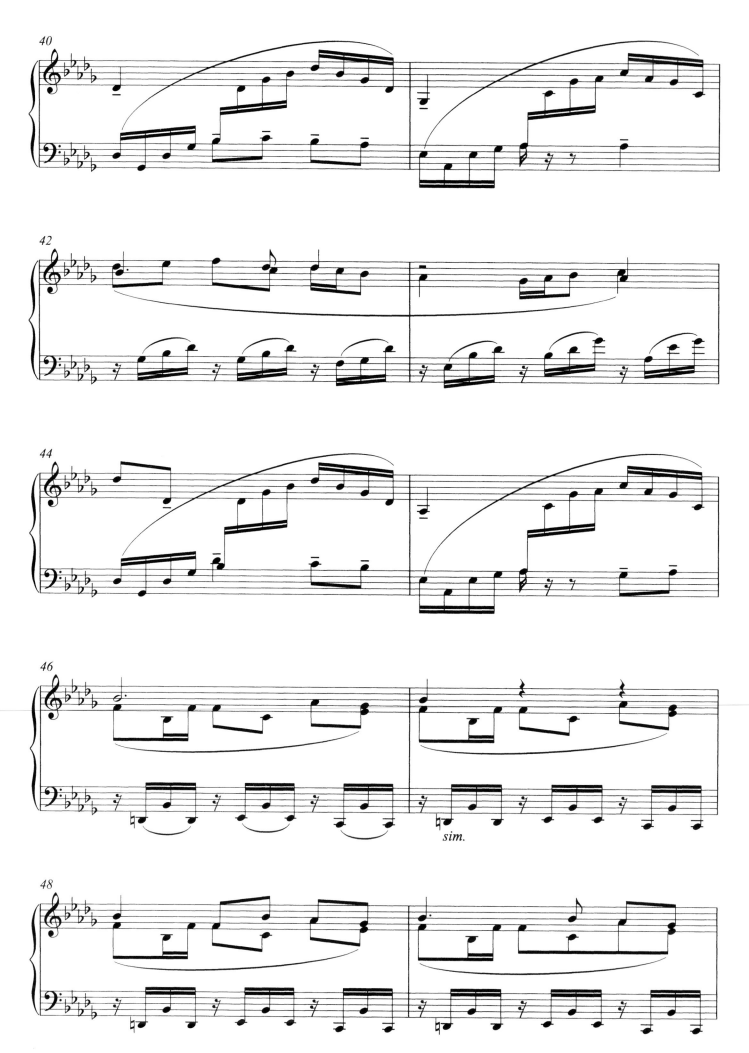

Les roses d'Ispahan
Op.39, No.4

Composed by Gabriel Fauré

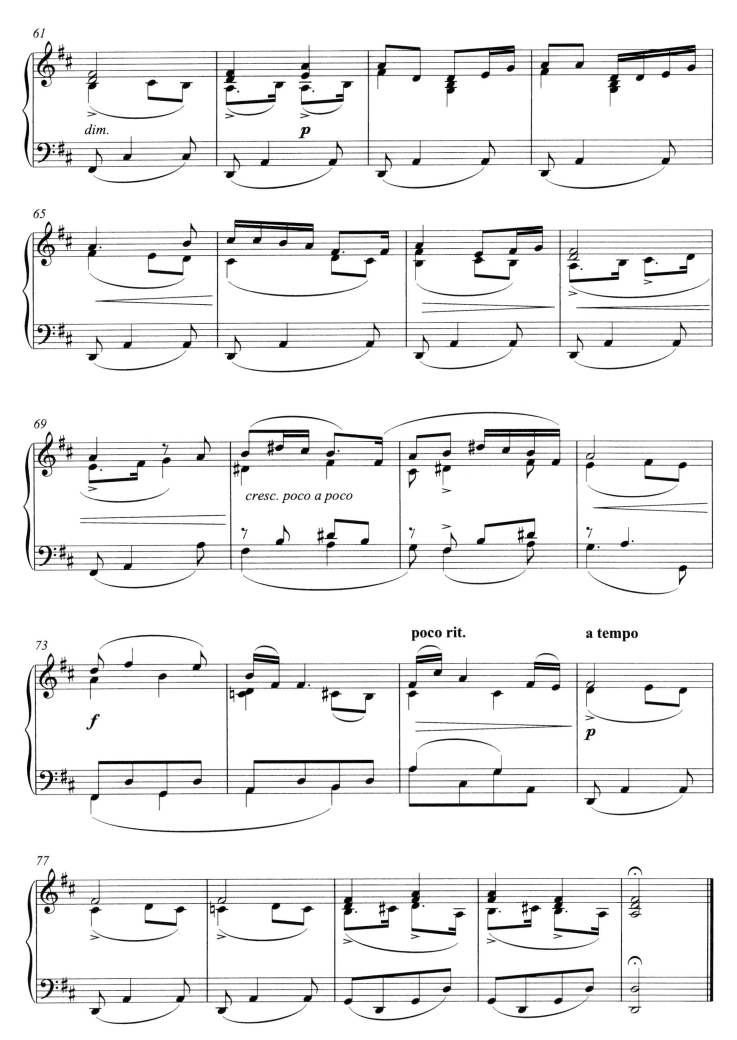

Poème d'un jour: Adieu
Op.21, No.3

Composed by Gabriel Fauré

Moderato ♩ = 76

Berceuse
(from The Dolly Suite)
Op.56

Composed by Gabriel Fauré

Andantino moderato

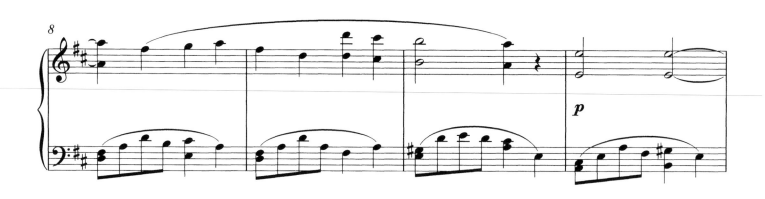

Tendresse
(from The Dolly Suite)
Op.56

Composed by Gabriel Fauré

Barcarolle No.1 in A Minor

(extract)
Op.26

Composed by Gabriel Fauré

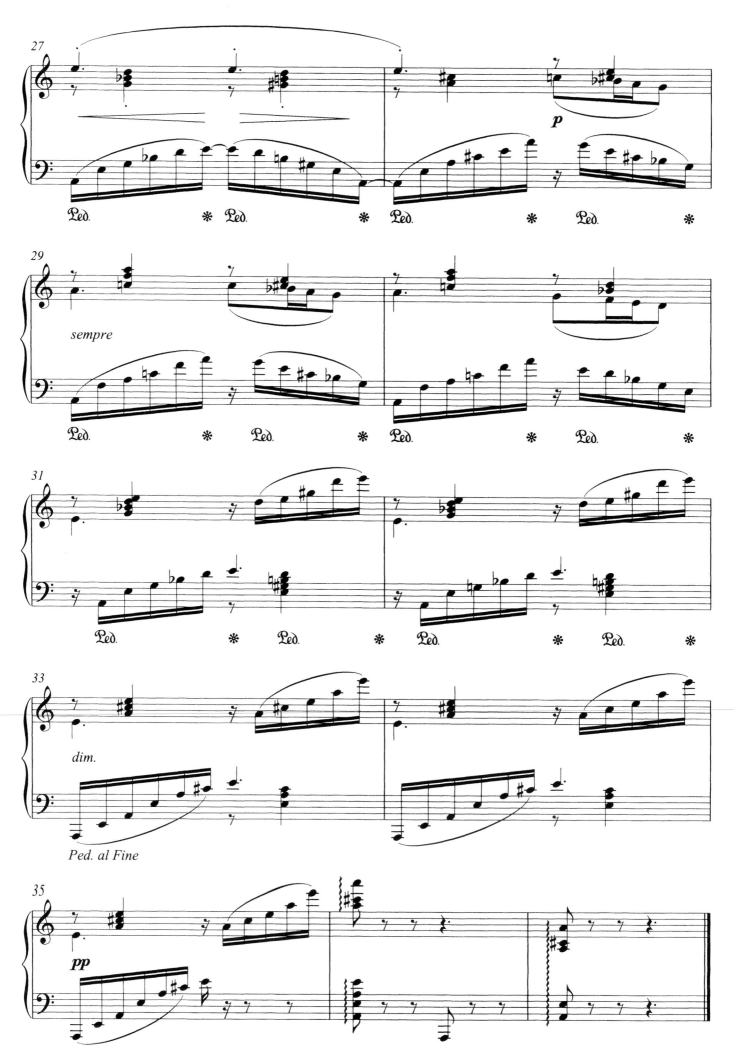

Barcarolle No.4 in A♭ Major
Op.44

Composed by Gabriel Fauré

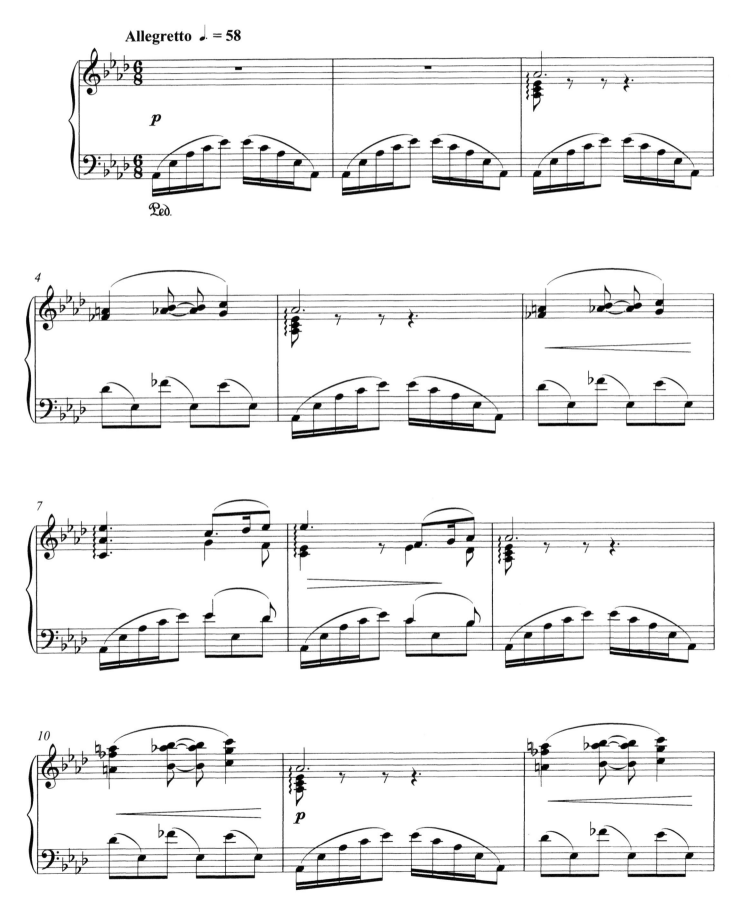

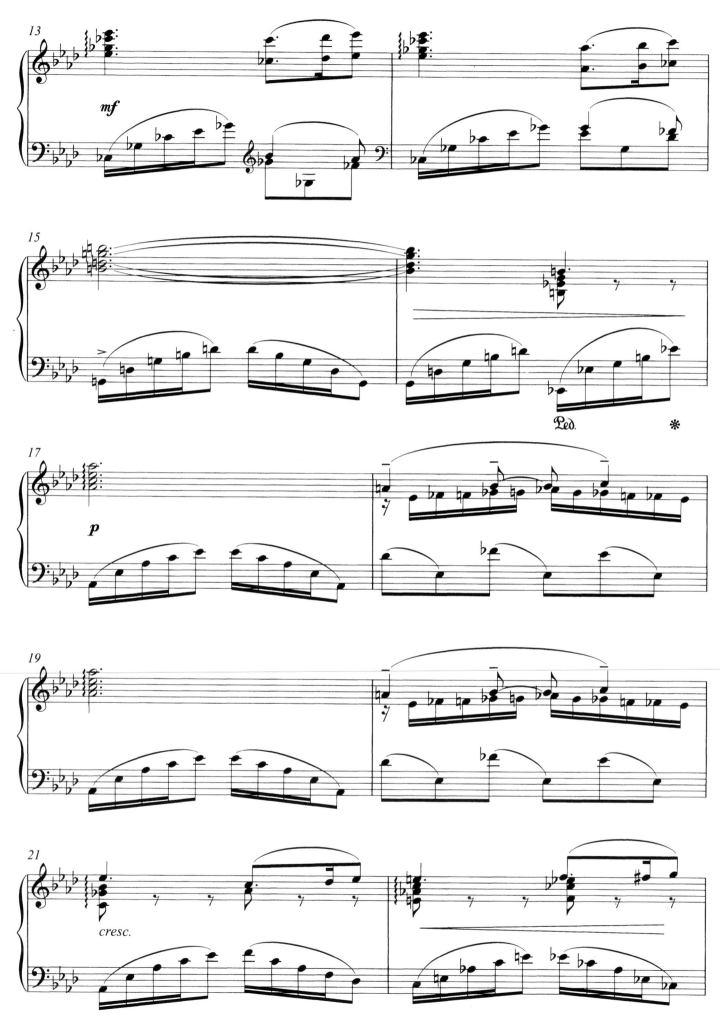

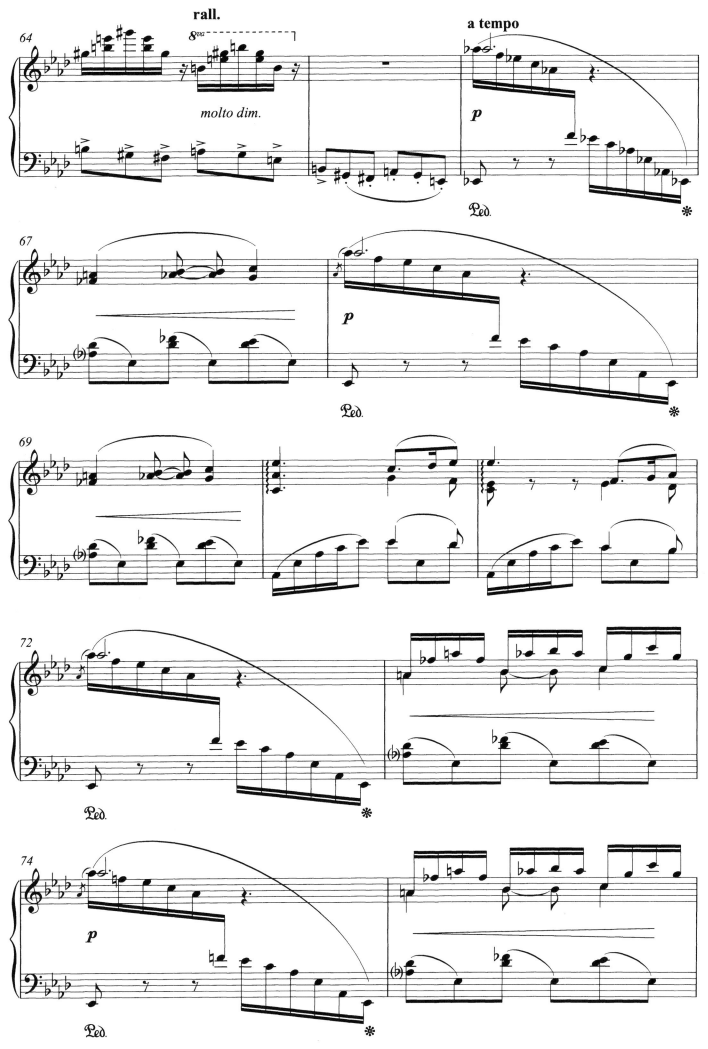

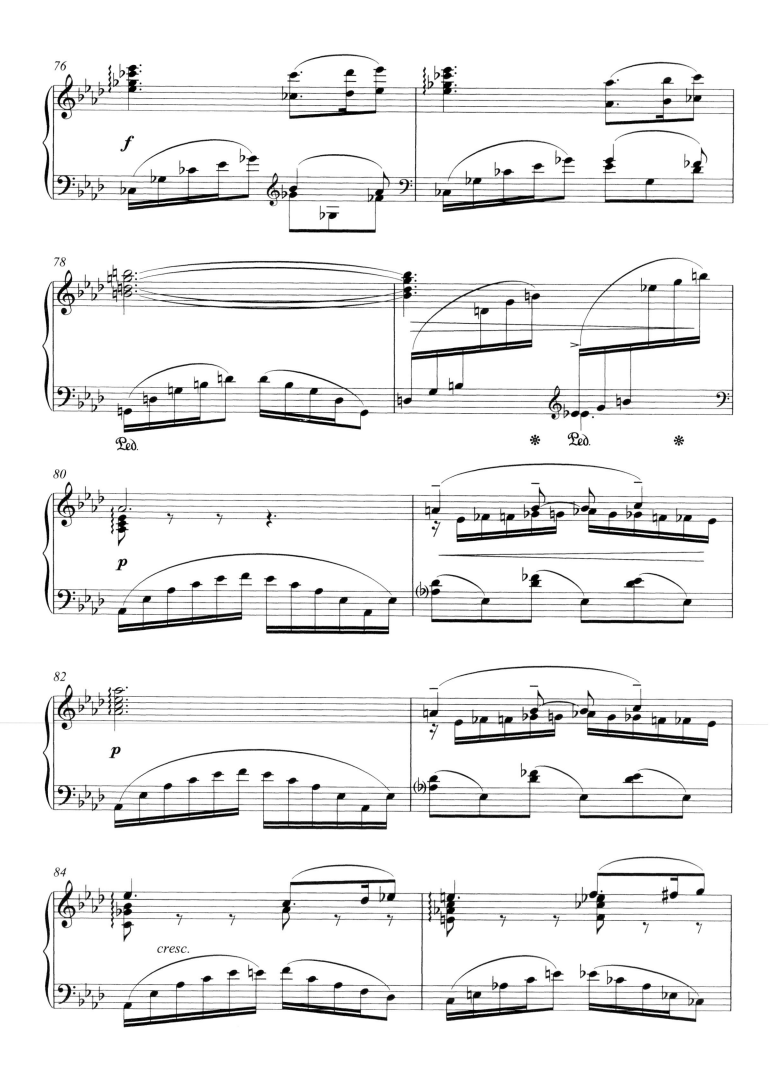

Nocturne No.1 in E♭ Minor
(extract)
Op.33

Composed by Gabriel Fauré

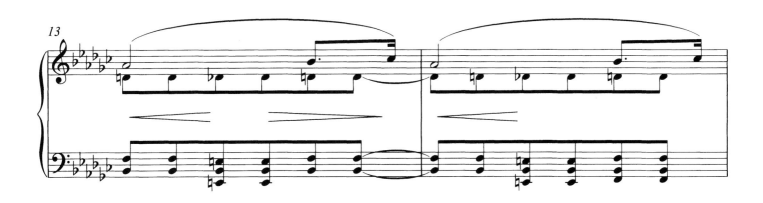

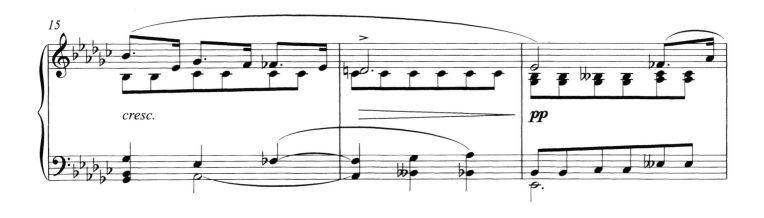

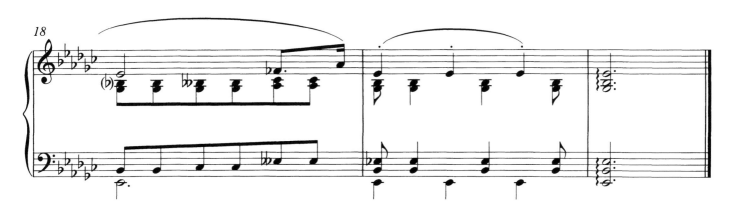

Nocturne No.5 in B♭ Major
(Andante quasi allegretto)
Op.37

Composed by Gabriel Fauré

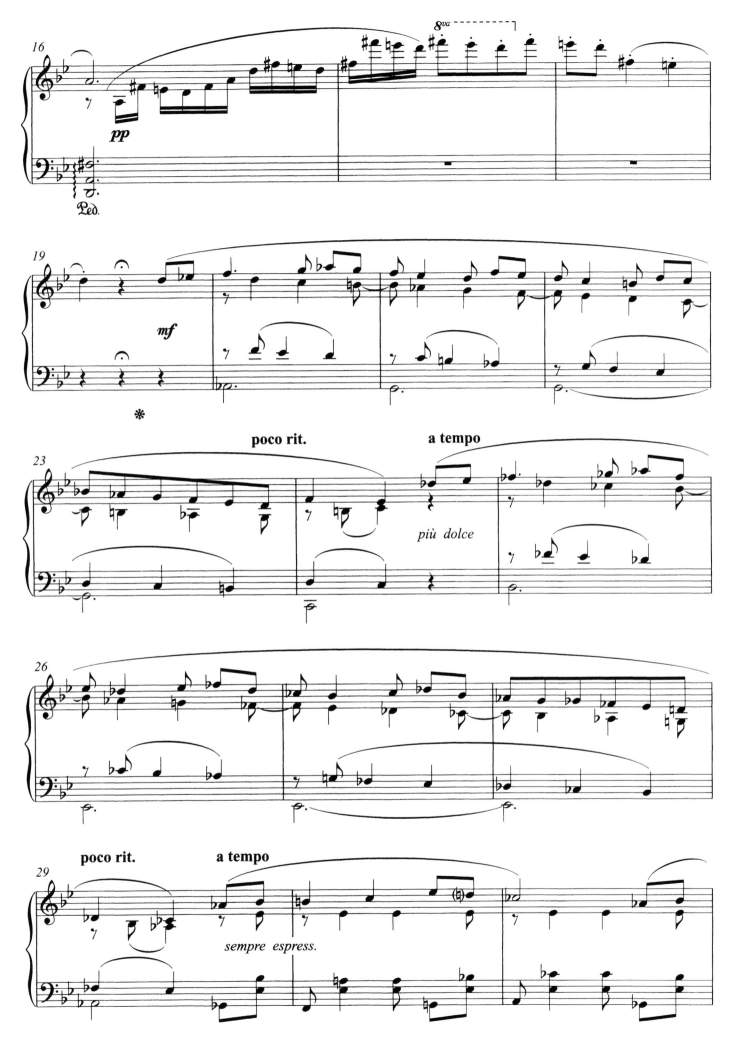

Prelude No.4 in F Major

Composed by Gabriel Fauré

Prelude No.9 in E Minor

Composed by Gabriel Fauré

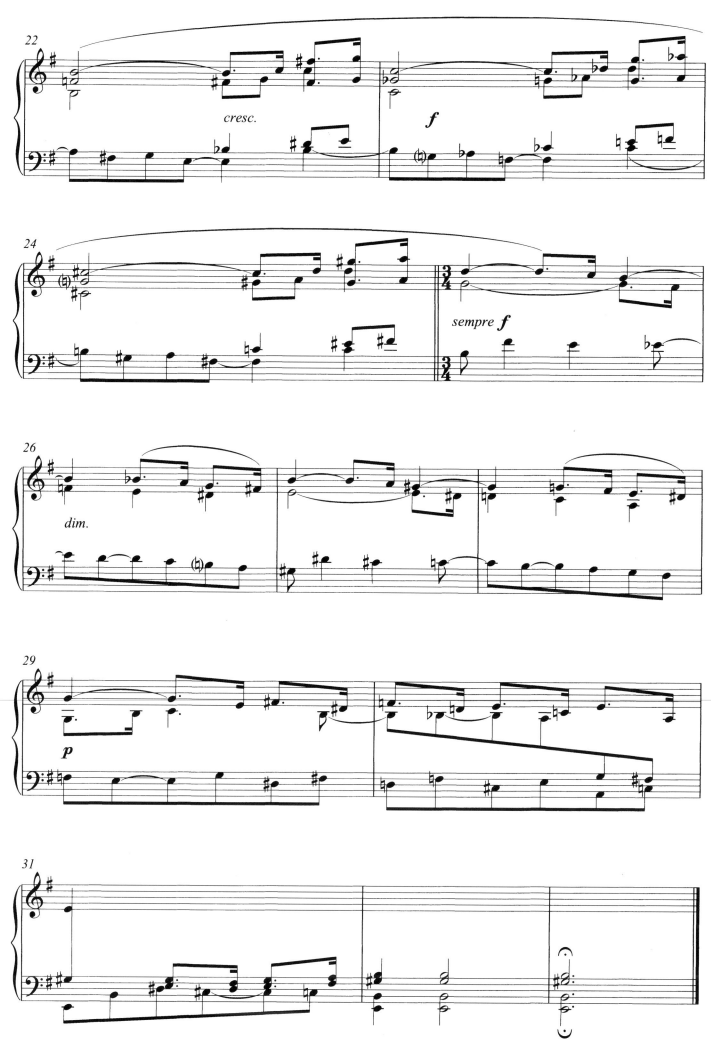

Song Without Words
Op.17, No.1

Composed by Gabriel Fauré

rit.   a tempo

Song Without Words
Op.17, No.3

Composed by Gabriel Fauré

Andante moderato ♩ = 76

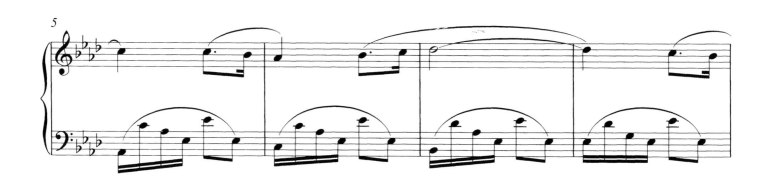

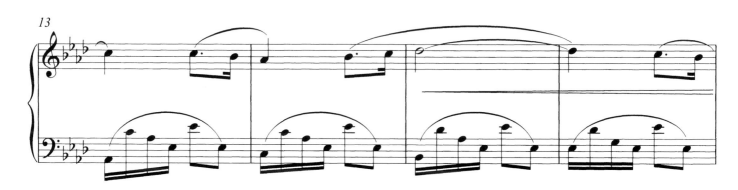

Impromptu No.3 in A♭ Major
(Allegro)
Op.34

Composed by Gabriel Fauré

Valse-Caprice No.1 in A Major
(Allegro moderato)
Op.30

Composed by Gabriel Fauré

Cantique de Jean Racine
Op.11

Composed by Gabriel Fauré

Agnus Dei
(from Requiem)
Op.48

Composed by Gabriel Fauré

Pie Jesu
(from Requiem)
Op.48

Composed by Gabriel Fauré

Sanctus
(from Requiem)
Op.48

Composed by Gabriel Fauré

Berceuse
Op.16

Composed by Gabriel Fauré

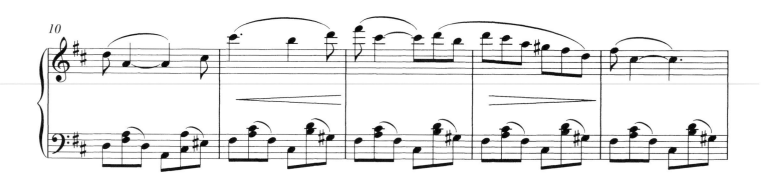

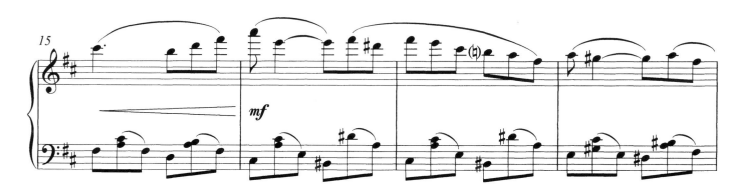

Pavane
Op.50

Composed by Gabriel Fauré

Andante molto moderato

Elégie

(extract)

Op.24

Composed by Gabriel Fauré

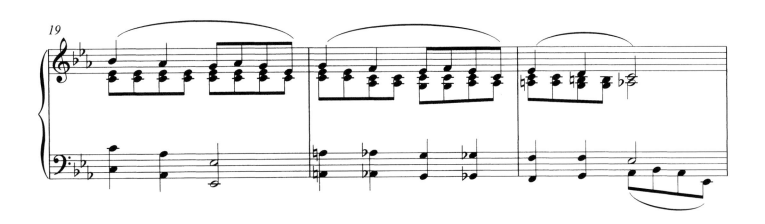

Sicilienne
(from Pelléas et Mélisande)
Op.80

Composed by Gabriel Fauré

Gabriel Fauré

The French composer Gabriel Fauré (1845-1924) is often dismissed as a salon composer, best known for small forms such as songs and short piano pieces. However, he was the most advanced composer of his generation, writing music that was unmistakeably French but uniquely personal, especially in its use of harmony. His music embodies order and restraint, with clear texture and form.

Fauré was born on 12th May 1845, the youngest of six children. In 1854 he was sent to the École Niedermeyer in Paris, to train as a choirmaster and organist. One of his teachers was the composer Camille Saint-Saëns, who influenced him enormously. The training he received in the polyphonic music of the Renaissance era, plainsong and Church Modes (scales that are not major or minor but have different arrangements of tones and semitones) was crucial to his later style. He liked to create ambiguity between major and minor chords, and often flattened the leading-note in a key, creating a modal effect. Some of his earliest compositions, the *Songs Without Words*, are included in this album, as is a transcription of the *Cantique de Jean Racine* for chorus and orchestra, for which he won the composition prize on leaving the École Niedermeyer in 1865.

In 1871 Fauré formed the Société Nationale de Musique with fellow composers d'Indy, Lalo, Duparc and Chabrier, in order to champion French music. In 1874 he joined the music staff at the Madeleine church in Paris. In 1883 he married Marie Fremiet, with whom he had two sons. With a family to support Fauré needed to continue with the work he found tedious, namely his job at the Madeleine and teaching piano and harmony. There was little time for composing except in the summer holidays and he was extremely self-critical of his work and often depressed.

Nevertheless, Fauré's piano music from the 1880s is elegant and captivating. Influenced by Mendelssohn and Chopin, the music is lyrical rather than virtuosic. Many of the piano works in this album date from this period, including the first and fifth of his 13 Nocturnes, the first and fourth of his 13 Barcarolles, the third of five Impromptus and the first of four Valse-Caprices.

Fauré has been called the greatest master of French song, writing nearly 100 throughout his life. *Après un rêve* (1878) is Italian in style, while *Clair de lune* of 1887 was a setting of a poem by Verlaine, a poet whose work he set with great success, conveying atmosphere and feeling rather than specific images. During this period he also composed the enduringly popular *Pavane* (1887).

In the 1890s Fauré finally began to realise some of his ambitions. In 1896 he was promoted to chief organist at the Madeleine and succeeded Massenet as teacher of composition at the Paris Conservatoire of Music, where his pupils included Ravel. He finally achieved success with larger scale works, mostly incidental music for plays, and in 1900 he finished the orchestrated version of his *Requiem*, which he had begun composing in 1877.

The work is a hauntingly beautiful setting of the Latin Requiem Mass, set for choir, organ and orchestra with soprano and baritone soloists. Fauré's characteristic unfolding of a melody, making much use of one or two melodic and rhythmic ideas, is clearly heard in both the 'Sanctus' and the 'Agnus Dei', transcribed for this album. The lines are spun out with an inevitability and sense of direction that is not interrupted by his sudden key-changes and often ambiguous harmony. Also included is the famous soprano solo 'Pie Jesu', a beautifully simple melody over a gentle accompaniment. Other famous works of this time include the haunting *Elégie* (1896) for cello and orchestra, and his *Dolly* suite for piano duet (1894-7).

In 1905 Fauré became director of the Paris Conservatoire and finally achieved fame and recognition. The latter period of his life was his most productive, despite deafness and distortion that affected his perception of the highest and lowest sounds. His compositions gained more expressive force, with bold harmony. His nine Preludes for piano date from this time, and the fourth and ninth are included here.

In 1920 Fauré retired from the Conservatoire a celebrity and was finally free to concentrate on composition. He was awarded the Grand Croix of the Légion d'Honneur, an unprecedented honour for a musician, and was much admired by younger French composers.

In his last years he concentrated on composing some extremely fine chamber music. He was in poor health for the last two years of his life and died in Paris on 4th November 1924. He had linked the end of the Romantic era in France with the 'modern' style emerging in the twentieth century, and remained the most technically advanced French composer until Debussy.

Kate Bradley
August 2004